Arthur Henry Bullen

Pimlico

1609

Arthur Henry Bullen

Pimlico
1609

ISBN/EAN: 9783744723145

Printed in Europe, USA, Canada, Australia, Japan

Cover: Foto ©Andreas Hilbeck / pixelio.de

More available books at **www.hansebooks.com**

ANTIENT DROLLERIES.

(No. 2.)

𝔓imlyco, or, 𝔎unne 𝔎ed=𝔠ap.

TIS A MAD WORLD AT HOGSDON.

1609.

REPRODUCED IN FACSIMILE

BY

THE OXFORD UNIVERSITY PRESS,

WITH A PREFACE

BY

A. H. BULLEN.

OXFORD:

PRINTED FOR PRIVATE CIRCULATION.

1891.

PREFACE.

HOGSDON, or HOXTON, a not very cheerful quarter of the town to-day, was formerly a favourite resort of holiday-makers. It was noted for cakes, custards, and " Pimlico " ale.

The origin of the name " Pimlico " has been discussed from time to time in *Notes and Queries*, but more light is still needed. It is usually stated that a person named Pimlico kept a place of entertainment at Hoxton, and that the place was afterwards called by his name. In the first volume of the first series of *Notes and Queries* Edward F. Rimbault quoted from *Newes from Hogsdon*, 1598,— " Have at thee [*sic*] then, my merrie boyes, and hey for old Ben Pimlico's nut browne." I have never seen the *Newes* (which Rimbault described as unique); and I should have been inclined to regard the quotation as spurious if Rimbault had not expressly stated that he wrote with the tract before him. In early seventeenth century plays there are many references to the place Pimlico, and to Pimlico ales ; but I cannot recall any mention of Ben Pimlico.

On 15th April 1609 "a book called *Pimlico or Runne Red Capp* tis a mad world at *Hogsden*" was

entered by the publisher John Busby in the Stationers'
Register (Arber's *Transcript*); and on 24th April the
same publisher entered "a ballad called *Haue with
you to Pimlico.*" Both the book and the ballad were
transferred on 3rd May to William Barley. The
ballad may be extant, but I have never seen it;
the "book" is here reproduced, among our *Antient
Drolleries*, for the amusement of curious readers.

The anonymous writer describes with much gusto
how people of every degree flocked to Hogsden to
drink the Pimlico ales. Play-goers deserted the
Fortune and the Bull for the attractions of Pimlico:—

> "Each afternoone thy House being full,
> Makes Fortune blind, or Gelds The Bull." (SIG. D. 2.)

In 1609, when our tract appeared, Pimlico seems
to have reached the height of its prosperity; for in
1610 Ben Jonson, in *The Alchemist* (v. 1), speaks of
its notoriety as a thing of the past:—

> "Gallants, men and women,
> And of all sorts, tag-rag, been seen to flock here
> In threaves, these ten weeks, as to a second Hogsden,
> In days of Pimlico and Eye-bright [1]."

But for many years afterwards, as we learn from
the pages of Shirley, Jasper Mayne, Glapthorne, &c.,

---

[1] "Eyebright" is mentioned in our tract:—

> "Eyebright, (so fam'd of late for Beere)
> Although thy Name be numbred heere,
> Thine ancient Honors now runne low;
> Thou art struck blind by Pimlyco."

Pimlico continued to be a place of entertainment. A correspondent of *Notes and Queries* (6th Series, 9, 296) quoted from *A New Dictionary of the Terms, Ancient and Modern, of the Canting Crew* (n. d., early eighteenth century),—" Pimlico.—A noted Cake-house formerly, but now converted into a Bowling-green of good repute at Hogsden near London." To this day the name is preserved in Pimlico Walk, a narrow alley leading from High Street, Hoxton, to the Church [1].

If I were in the mood for annotation, the little tract here reproduced would afford ample opportunities; but I refrain. In this short series of *Antient Drolleries* I propose to give mere reprints of quaint out-of-the-way tracts. The series will, I trust, be useful to those who are studying or editing Elizabethan Writers. Shakespearean editors may notice that the present tract testifies to the popularity of *Pericles* (printed in the same year, 1609) :—

> "(As at a New-play) all the Roomes
> Did swarme with Gentiles mix'd with Groomes.
> So that I truly thought, all These
> Came to see *Shore*, or *Pericles*." (SIG. C.)

---

[1] The Pimlico in the West is of later date than Pimlico, Hoxton. Cunningham gives some extracts from the books of the overseers of the poor for St. Martin's in the Fields, dated 1626 to 1630; and these are said to supply the earliest notices of the Western Pimlico. There is a hamlet named Pimlico in Oxfordshire, and there is (or was) a Pimlico in Dublin. A small West Indian island bears the name; and in Barbadoes there was " a strange bird the Pemlico, which presageth storms."

Shore is, I suppose, Heywood's *Edward IV.*

Pimlico is a rare tract. Our reprint is from the copy[1] in the Malone collection, Bodleian library. Malone's is the only copy that I know, but probably others are extant. There was a copy among the books that Robert Burton (Democritus Junior) bequeathed to the Bodleian, but it seems to have disappeared. I know not what became of Heber's copy.

169, *New Bond Street, London,*
    14th August, 1891.

---

[1] I thought there would be no harm in reproducing the portrait of Elinour Rummin (which is bound up with Malone's copy) from the 1624 edition of Skelton's well-known poem.

ELINOVR RVMMIN,

The famous Ale-wife of *England*.

Written by Mr. *Skelton*, Poet Laureat to King

Henry the egiht

When Skelton *wore the Lawrell Crowne,*
My Ale put all the Ale-wiues downe.

LONDON

Printed for *Samuel Rand* 1624.

PIMLYCO.

Or,

Runne Red-Cap.

Tis a mad world at *Hogsdon*.

At London,

¶ *Printed for Jo: Busbie, and Geo:*
Loftis, and are to bee sould vnder S^t.
Peters Church in Cornehill. 1609.
(*⁎*)

Patrono Pimlyconico.

Facie Claro,
Facetijs Raro,
Thoma Normano.

ALL hayle, (ò *Tom Norman*,)
I make thee, the *Foreman*
  Of *Pimlyco* Iury:
You are chargde to enquire Sir,
What kindles that fire fir,
  That burnes with such fury.
What fire doe you suppose fir?
Tis the fire of your *Nose* fir,
  Which your *Face* beares about.
For (like to the fornace,
That glowes in the *Glasse-house*,)
  It neuer goes out.
To keepe that hye *Colour*,
And make it looke fuller,
  You shall die it in graine fir:
Of the *Pimlyco* Iuice,
If you get the right vfe,
  O how well will it staine fir.
I create you *Sole Patron*
Of the *Pimlyco Squadron*
  choose therefore *Ale-cunners*.
That now against *Easter*,
(If you purpose to feast there)
  may be your fore-runners:
Hoyst then vp your Sayle fir,
For rich *Pimlyco* Ale fir,
  That cullors like *Roses*,
With your Copper *Seale*, marke fir,
All those that Embarke fir,
  For *Pimlyco-Nofes*.

Vade, Vale, Caue ne titubes.

To all Trauellers.

*Y*ou that weare out your liues and weary your bodies, in Discouery of strange Countries, (bee it for pleasure or profite)Rig out a Fleet,and make a Voiage to an Iland which could neuer be found out by the Portugals,Spaniards, or Hollanders,but only (and that now of late) by Englishmen. The name of it is Pimlyco, Here haue I drawne a large Map of it: by this Chart, may you in a few houres, and with little or no winde, ariue in the very mouth of the Hauen. Some that haue trauelled thither,affirme it to be a part of the Continent, but the better sort of Nauigators say, it is an Iland: full of people it is, and they are very wilde, the women beeing able to endure more, and to doe better Seruice than the men. Diuers are of opinion, that it is an inchanted Iland; and haunted with strange Spirits;for the people there,once euery Moone, are either starke mad, or else loose their owne shapes, and are transformed into Beasts,yet within twelue houres, recouer their wittes and shapes againe. The Pimlyconians are most of them Malt-men, and exceeding good fellowes, all their delight beeing in Eating and Drinking; they liue not long, for a man can hardly stay amongest them two dayes: if he doe, he is in great danger, by reason of a certaine disease, (which the Iland naturally breedes) called the Staggers, through which, many of them come to their Downe-fall, or if they scape that,then are they in feare to be made away by Small-shot, in discharging of which, the Pimlyconians are very actiue and cunning.

The

To all Trauellers.

The Iland *begins now to be as rich as it is populous: fish hath bin seldome taken there , but flesh is better cheape then* Mackrell *here. Wilde* Duckes *and wilde* Geese *flie there vp and downe in aboundance: you may haue a* Goose *sowc'd in* Pimlyco, *for the value of twelue pence sterling. Woodcockes (in many moneths of the yeere) are to be catched there by whole dozens. It is full of fatte pasture, and thats the reason such multitudes of* young Colts *runne there. A* hot Climate *it is, and by that meanes the people are subiect to infection, which takes them first in the* Head, *and so falls downe into their legges, and those fayling, they are (in a maner) gone. The* Gouernour *of the* Iland *hath much adoe to* keepe himselfe *vpright, so that he is compelled to giue those that are vnder him, often times very* Hard *measure, yet are they so vnruly, that euery houre one or other goes to the* Pot,*

Thus haue I giuen you a taste, both of the People *and of the* Countrie; *if you sayle thither, you may drinke of deeper knowledge: But take heed you take a skilfull* Pilot *with you ; be fraighted with as much wit as you can carry aboord, for all will be little enough to bring you from thence, and take heede what* Lading *you take in there, for the commodities of* Pimlyco *haue suncke many* Merchants. *Pay thankes for my* Councell, *and thinke well of my* Pimlyconian Discouerie.

Farewell.

Pimlyco.

Rees that of late (like wasted Heyres,
Or like old men, dryed vp with cares,)
Stwd poorely, now looke fresh & greene,
As Banck-rupts new set vp agen.
Medowes that whilome barren lay,
(More naked than the trodden way,)
Weare garments now, wouen all of Flowers,
And waite on Flora in her Bowers,
Shepheards that durst not, (for the cold,)
The Snowie heads of Hills behold,
Now (deftly piping) from coole Fountaines,
Lead Lambes and Kiddes vp to the Mountaines.
The Day, when all Birdes hold their Weddings,
(Dauncing Loue-measures in soft Treddings,)
Is past: The Yeare did it resigne,
In honour of Saint Valentine.
And now his Fethered Couples sing,
Their Nuptiall Songs before the Spring.
The Vernall Gates are set wide open,
And strew'd with Flowers and Herbes, in token
That May (Loues Queene) is comming in,
Who 12. full Moones hath absent bin.
In this Sweet Season, from my bed,
I earely rose, being wakened
By'th beating of a Golden flame,
Which (to me) in at window came.
For from his Pallace in the East,
The King of Light in Purple drest,
(Set thicke with Gold and precious Stone,
Which like a Rocke of Diamond shonne,)

Description of the Spring.

Description of the Sun-rising.

B   Was

Pimlyco.

Was drawne along heab'ns Siluer way,
By the 4. Horses of the Day.
And as the Chariot mounted higher,
The Sun-god sæm'd to ride in fire,
Forth came he in this braue adorning.
To court his Loue (the Rosie Morning.)
The Chaines of Pearle about her necke,
He tooke from her himselfe to decke,
They were her fauours and he woze them
Till night, and did agen restoze them.
The wonders (of vn-valued worth,)
Which these two wrought, intic'd mee forth;
Weary with walking, downe J threw
My bodie, on a bancke where grew
The pretty Dazie, (Eye of Day,)
The Prime-Rose which does first display
Her youthfull colours, and first dies ;
   ,, Beautie and Death are Enemies.
Cowslips sprung likewise here and there,
Each blade of grasse (stiffe as a Speare)
Standing vpright to guard the Flowers,
As if they had bæn their Paramoures,
Anon a Yonker and his Lasse,
Right J sæ wrastling on the Grasse,
Shæ swoze shæ would not fall, and yet
Shæ fell, and did a Greene-Gowne get,
(A Greene-gowne, but no Gowne of Greene.)
At length (in Couples) moze were sæne:
Som ran, some walked, and some sat kissing.
Nothing was lost, but what was missing
So close they ioynd in their Delights,
That they all sæm'd Hermaphrodites,
Or rather Mermaides on the land,
Because the Shees had th'vpper hand.
They grac'd the fields, the fields them grac's,
For tho none were in ozder plac'de,
But sat (as Flowers in Gardens grow)
Thinly, which makes the brauer show.

Yet

Pimlyco.

Yet (like so many in one Roome,)
All sæm'd to weaue within a loome,
Some curious piece whose beautie stands,
on the rare Skill of sundry hands.

As thus they sat, and I them saw,
A Frame (as rare) mine eies did draw
(With wonder) to behold a farre,
The brightnes of the Kingdomes * Starre;   * London.
A thousand Stæples, Turrets, Towers,
(Lodgings, all fit for Emperours,)
Lifted their proud heads boue the Skie,
As if they had sole Soueraigntie,
Or'e all the Buildings in the Land,
And sæm'd on Hilles of Gould to stand,
For the Suns Beames on them being shed,
They shewed like Mynes new burnished.
Upon the Left hand and the Right,   * Islington, &
Two * Townes (like Citties) fed the Sight,   Hogsdon.
With pleasure and with admiration,
For (as they stand) they beare proportion,
As to an Armie doe the Wings,
(The maine Battalion led by Kings.)

Mine eye his obiects could not bary,
Yet tooke delight here still to tarry,
But not knowing how to weare out time,
By chance I found a Booke in Ryme,   Skelton.
Writ in an age when few wryt well,
(Pans Pipe (where none is) does excell.)
O learned Gower! It was not thine,
Nor Chaucer, (thou art more Diuine.)
To Lydgates graue I should do wrong,
To call him vp by such a Song.
No, It was One, that (boue his Fate,)
Would be Styl'd Poet Laureate;
Much like to Some in these our daies,
That (as bold Prologues do to Playes,)
With Garlonds haue their Fore-heads bound,
Yet onely empty Sculles are crownde:

Pimlyco.

Or like to these (sæing others hye)
Will sit so, tho their Seate they buy,
And fill it vp with loathed Scorne,
Fit Burdens being by them not borne,
But sæing their Trappings rich and gay,
The Sumpter-Horses trudge away,
Sweating themselues to death to beare them,
When poore Iades (drawing the Plough) outweare
   But all this while we haue forgot   (them.
Our Poet: tho I nam'de him not,
But only should his Rymes recite,
These (all would cry) did Skelton wrife.
I tournde some leaues and red them o're,
And at last spyed his Elynor,
His Elynor, whose fame spred saile,
All England through for Nappy Ale.
Elynor Rumming warmde his wit
With Ale, and his Rimes paide for it.
But sæing thou tak'st the Laureats name
(Skelton) I iustly thée may blame,
Because thou leau'st the Sacred Fount,
For Liquor of so base account.
Yet (I remember) euen the Prince
Of Poesie, with his pen (long since)
Ledde to a Fielde, the Mice and Frogges;
Others haue ball'd out bookes of Dogges:
Our diuine Maro spent much oyle
About a Gnat. One képs a coyle
With a poore Flea (Naso, whose wit
Brought him by Phœbus side to sit.)
Since then these Rare-ones slack'd their strings,
From the hie-tuned acts of Kings
For notes so low, lesse is thy Blame,
For in their pardon stands thy Name.
Let's therefore lead our eyes astray,
And from our owne intended way,
Go backe to view thine Hostesse picture,
Whom thus thou draw'st in liuely coloure.
                        Skeltons

Pimlyco.

❧ Skeltons tunning of *Elynor Rumming.*

Tell you I chill,
If that you will
A while be still,
Of a comely Iyll,
That dwelt on a hill,
But shee is not grill,
For shee is somwhat sage,
And well worne in age,
For her vilage
It would asswage
A mans corage.

    Her loathly leare
Is nothing cleare
But ugly of cheare.
Droopy and drowsy,
Scuruey and lowsy,
Her face all bowsy,
Comely crinckled,
Wondersly wrinckled,
Like a roast Pigs eare
Bristled with heare.

    Her lewd lippes twaine.
They Slauer men sayen,
Like a ropy rayne,
A gummy glayre:
Shee is ugly faire,
Her nose some=deale hooked
And camously crooked,

Pimlyco.

Neuer stopping,
But euer dropping
Her Skin loose and slacke,
Grayned like a Sacke,
With a crooked backe.

Her eyen gowndy,
Are full, vnsowndy,
For they are bleared,
And shee gray heared,
Iawed like a Ietty,
A man would haue pitty,
To see how shees gummed,
Fingerd and thumbed;
Gentlye Ioynted,
Greased and annointed,
Up to the knuckles,
The bones her buckles,
Together made fast,
Her youth is far past:
Footed like a Plane,
Legges like a Crane,
And yet shee will Iet,
Like a Iolly Set,
In her fur'd flocket
And gray russet rocket,
With Simper the cocket.

Her Huke of Lincolne greene,
It had beene hers I weene,
More than fortie yeare,
And so it doth appeare:
And the greene bare threds
Looke like Sere weedes,
Withered like hay,

The

Pimlyco.

The wooll worne away,
And yet I dare say,
Shee thinks her selfe gay
Upon the holliday,
When shee doth her array,
And girdeth in her getes,
Stitched & prancked with pletes:
Her kirtle Bristow red,
With cloaths vppon her head,
That they wey a sowe of lead,
Writhen in a wonder wise,
After the Sarazens gise,
With a whim wham,
Knit with a trim tram,
Vpon her braine pan
Like an Egiptian,
Capped about,
When shee goeth out,
Her selfe for to shew,
Shee draweth downe the dew,
With a paire of heeles,
As broad as two wheeles,
Shee hobbles as shee goes,
With her blancket hose,
Her shoone smeard with tallow,
Greased vppon di t,
That daubeth the Skirt.
              Primus Passus.
And this comely Dame,
I vnderstand her name
Is Elynor Rumming,
At home in her wonning:
And as men say

                              Shee

Pimlyco.

Shee dwelt in Sothray,
Jn a certen ſtede
Beſide Lederhede,
Shee is a tonniſh gib,
The Deuill and ſhee be Sib.

I Ked and ſmilde, but at the laſt,
As toward the towne mine eye J caſt,
Jn mingled trœpes J might beholde
Women and men (ſome yong, ſome olde)
Like to a Spring-tide, ſtrongly flowing
To Hogsdon, not one backward going.
Out of the Citty ruſh'd the ſtreame,
A while (me thought) J did but dreame,
That J ſaw people, till at laſt,
Hogſdon ore-flowde, it ſwel'd ſo faſt.
J muſde that from the Citty venturde
Such heapes : for tho the Spring was enterde,
They flock'd not thus to heare the Tune
Of that bird who ſings beſt in Iune,
(Yclip'd the Cuckoe) as yet her note
Shee had not perfect, but by rote :
Ne durſt ſhæ ſing yet, being not able
Jn Engliſh, but in —— to gabble.
Nor was it like they made theſe throngs,
To heare the Nightingals ſad ſongs,
For Luſt (in theſe dayes) beares ſuch price,
They are but mock'd that checke that Vice.
    Still more and more this Sea brake in,
Yet ebb'd in one halfe houre agen,
The Voyagers that firſt did Vaile,
(Hauing their Lading) homeward ſaile.
But with a ſloe-winde were they driuen,
Yet all caſt anchor in one Hauen.
Up went my ſailes, With much adœ,
Jn the ſame Port J anchorde tœ.
Being landed there, all J could finde

Was

Pimlyco.

Was this, They came to hunt the Hinde.
 Into their Parke I forthwith went,
Being entred, all the ayre was rent
With a most strange confused noyse,
That sounded nothing but mære voyce.
Amazde I stood to sæ a Crowd
Of Ciuill Throats stretch'd out so lowd:
(As at a New-play) all the Roomes
Did swarme with Gentiles mir'd with Groomes.
So that I truly thought, all These
Came to sæ Shore, or Pericles,
And that (to haue themselues well plac'd)
Thus brought they vicualls (they fed so fast)
But then (agen mæ thought) This shoale
Swom thither for Bakers doale
Or Brewers, and that for their soules sakes,
They thus were seru'd with Ale and cakes:
For Iugs of Ale came rèling in,
As if the Pots had drunkards bin.
 A Tayler (that had narrow eyes
Through fumes that vp to his braines did rise)
Got I by th'arme, (children they say,
And Fooles and Drunkards, truth bewray)
Him therefore I desirde to show
Why all these met.——— Tis Pimlyco———
My Friend, Tis Pimlyco (hæ cryde)
And no worde could I get beside.
This made me madder then before,
I ask'd another, and hee swore
Zoundes——— I'me ten strong in Pimlyco———
What's that saide I?——— stowt Pimlyco———
And backe, at least thræ yardes hæ ræles,———
Pimlyco trips vp good mens heeles
(Lisping) he cryes, and downe he falls,
Yet for more Pimlyco——— still he calls.
 What Pimlyco should meane I wondred,
Because so lowd that word still thundred
From all their throats through all their eares,

      C   **R**

Pimlyco.

At length, a reuerend man (whose yeares
Had tourn'd his head and beard all gray,
And came but to beholde That Play,
And not to act himselfe The Vice)
Tolde all the Dronken Misteries.
And that the Ale got such high Fame,
Only by that fond, sencelesse Name.
   I laugh'd to see a World(so wise,
So subtile in all Villanies,
So scorning to be laugh'd to scorne)
Should be so drownde with Ale in Corne
Yet since in Hogsdon all ran mad,
I playde the Mad-man too, and had
My Iug brought in; a draught or twaine
Made such hot boyling in my braine,
That (faster then their Pots were filde)
From my Inuention were distilde
Verses in Pimlyco's high prayse,
Pimlyco crownde my head with bayes.
For straight I felt my selfe a Poet,
And (like some fooles) in Rime must show it.
Yet first I tournde o're Skeltons Rimes
With those mad times to weigh our Times,
And try how Elynor Rummings Ale.
Was Brew'd; and Drawne, and set to Sale,
What Guests drunk there, and what Drinke heere,
In this wilde Lantskip shall appeare.

But to make vp my tale,
  She brueth nappy Ale,
And maketh thereof poort sale,
To trauaplers, to tynkers,
To sweaters, to swinkers,
And all good Ale drinkers,
That will nothing spare,
But drinke till they stare,
            And

Pimlyco.

And bring them selues bare,
with now away the Mare,
And let vs slay care,
As wise as an hare.
　Come who so will
To Elynor on the hill,
with fill the Cup fill,
And sit thereby still.
Early and late,
Thither commeth Kate,
Cisley and Sare,
with their legges bare,
And also their feet,
Hardly full vnsweet,
with their heeles dagged,
Their kirtles all to iagged,
Their smockes all to ragged,
with titters and tatters,
Bring dishes and platters,
with all their might running,
To Elynor Rumming,
To haue of her Tunning,
Shee leaueth them of the hame,
And thus beginneth the game.
　Some wenches come vnbraced,
with their naked pappes,
That flippes and flappes,
It wigges and it wagges,
Like tawney Saffron bagges,
A sort of fowle drabbes,
All scuruy with scabbes,
Some be fly bitten,
Some skewd as a kitten,

　　　　　C 2　　　　　Some

Pimlyco.

Some with a shooe clowte,
Binde their heads about,
Some haue no haire lace,
Their lockes about their face,
Their tresses vntrust,
All ful of vnlust,
Some looke strawry,
Some cawry mawry,
Full vntidy tegges,
Like rotten egges,
Such a lewd sort,
To Elinor resort,
From tyde to tyde;
Abide, abide,
And to you shalbe told,
How her Ale is sold,
To mawt and to molde.

Secundus Passus.

Some haue no monney,
That thither commy,
For their Ale to pay,
That is a shrewd aray.
Elinour sweared, nay
Yee shall not beare away
My Ale for nought
By him that me bought.
With hey dog hay,
Haue these dogges away,
With get me a staffe,
The swine eate my draffe,
Strike the hogs with a club, (tub,
They haue drunke vp my swilling
For be there neuer so much prease,
                                        These

Pimlyco.

These swine goe to the hye dese,
The sow with her pigges,
The Bore his taile wrigges
Against the hye bench,
With so, there is a stench,
Gather vp thou wench,
Seest thou not what is fall,
Take vp drit and all,
And beare out of the hall,
God giue it ill preuing,
Clenly as euill cheuing.

But let vs turne playne,
There wee left agayne,
For as ill a patch as that,
The hennes run in the mash fat,
For they goe to roust,
Strayt ouer the Ale ioust,
And dong when it comes
In the Ale tonnes,
Then Elinor taketh
The mash boll, and shaketh
The hennes dong away,
And skommeth it in a tray
where as the Pest is,
With her maungy fistis:
And sometimes she blens,
The dong of her hennes
And the Ale together,
And saith Gossip come hither,
This Ale shall be thicker,
And floure the more quicker,
For I may tell you,
I learned it of a Iew,

when

Pimlyco.

When I began to brew,
Drinke now while it is new.
And yee may it brooke,
It shall make you looke
Yonger than you bee
Yeeres two or three.
For yee may proue it by me,
Behold she said, and see,
How bright I am of blee,
Ich am not cast away,
That can my husband say,
When wee kisse and play,
In lust and in liking,
He calleth me his whyting,
His Mulling, and his Mittine
His Nobbes and his Cunny,
His sweeting and his honny,
With basse my pretty bonny,
Thou art worth good and monny,
This make I my falyre fanny,
Till that he Dreame and Dronny.
For after all our sport,
Than will hee ront and snort,
Then sweetly together we lye,
As two Pigges in a stye.
  But we will turne playne,
  where we left agayne.
    Tertius passus.
In stead of coyne and monny,
Some bring her a conny,
And some a pot with honny,
Some a salt, and some a spoone,
Some their hose, some their shoon.
                            Some

Pimlyco.

Some ran a good trot,
with a skillet oʒ a pot, &c.

*Cum multis alijs, quæ nunc perscribere lon-
gum est.*

Hoc est Skeltonicum,
Incipit Pimlyconicum.

Of Pimlyco now let vs sing,
Rich Pimlyco, the new-found Spʒing,
Where men and women both together,
To warme their vaines in froꝛy weather,
Where men and women hot blouds cœle,
By dʒincking Pimlycoes boyled poole.
Strong Pimlyco, the nouriſhing foode
To make men fat, and bʒæd pure blœd;
Deepe Pimlyco, the Well of Glee,
That dʒawes vp merry company.
Bewitching Pimlyco, that tyes
The Rich and Poore, the Foole and Wife,
All in one knot. Of that we wʒite ;
Inſpire your Poet to indite,
You Barlie Muſes Pimlyconian,
He ſcoʒnes the Muſes Helyconian;
(Pœʒe Soulest) they none but water dʒincke,
But Pimlyco dʒopt into his yncke,
His lines ſhall flye with merry gale,
No Muſe is like to Pimlyco Ale.
    Not the neat Wine De Orleans;
Noʒ of Hebrian, (beꝛ in France;)
Not Gafcoigne, noʒ the Burdeux Vine,
Noʒ that which ꝼowes from ſwiꝼ foote Rhyne;
Not Sheerys Sacks, noʒ Charnico,
Peter Semine, noʒ Mallago,
Noʒ th'Amber-colored Candie grape,
Which dʒuncke with Egges makes men to—Ape.
Noʒ can the Greekiſh Vintage ſhow

a

Pimlyco.

A liquoz matching Pimlyco.

Not Hipocras (the dzinke of women,)
Noz Ballards (that are deere, but common,)
Noz the fat lecherous Alligant,
Whose Juice repaires what Backes doe want.
Noz Waters dzawne by Diftillations,
With medcinable Operations,
As Rofa Solis, Aqua Vitæ,
And Nugs of Balme, fo quicke, and fpzighty;
No, noz the Irish Vfquebagh,
Of which, the Kerne whole ppntes will quaffe,
Strong Vfquebagh, that hotlier burnes
Than Sackes, and white the Entrailes turnes.
Noz welsh Metheglyn, (bzowne as berry)
Lancashier Syder, Wozstershier Perry,
Noz yet a dzaught of Darby Ale,
Noz mother Bunch, (long fince growne ftale,)
Noz that old two-peny Ale of Pynder,
That many a Pozter oft did hinder
From carrying Burdens, foz (alacke!)
The Ale had ftrength to bzeake his backe.
    Noz all thofe Dzinkes of Nozthzen Climes,
Whofe Bzewings shall fill bp our Rimes,
Brant, Renfque, and the clare Romayne,
The Belo, Crafno, and Patifane,
Pecua (to them as is our Beere,)
With fpiced Meades (wholfome, but deere)
As Meade Obarne, and Meade Cherunck,
And the bafe Quaffe bp Pefants dzunck.
With all the reft that whet the fpzites
Of Ruffes and cold Mufcouytes.
Not all thefe Drinkes, noz thowfand moe,
Can reach the fame of Pimlyco.
    To pzowe (ô Pimlyco) thefe thine honozs,
Armies each day fpzead Crimfon banners,
And with hye Colours, and quicke shot,
Fight ftifly till the field be got.
All Sexes, all Degrees, all Nations,

Pimlyco.

All men of Arts or Occupations,
(As if for gayne to some great Fayre,)
Onely for Ale to thœ repayre.
The English, Scottish, Dutch and French,
Sit whißling here vpon one bench:
If but of Pimlyco they drinke hard,
Betwixt them falls not one foule word,
They kisse like brothers, Dutch, French, Scot,
Are all One in a Pimlyco Pot.

   Hither come Sergeants with their Maces,
Hither come Bailiffes with red faces,
Hither come Lads and greaße Clownes,
Hither come pockets full of Crownes,
Hither come those can scarce find Baile
For sixe pence, yet spend eight in Ale.
Vsurers battle (here) their pence,
The Diuell can scarce keepe Brokers hence,
The Lawyer that in Terme-time takes
Fat fees, pleades here for Ale and Cakes.
Doctors, Proctors, Clarkes, Atturneis,
To Pimlyco make sweattie iournies,
And (being well Arm'd with Buckram bags,)
Fight vnder Hogsdons skarlet flags.
The Winde our Merchants this way driues,
Whilst their men take vp for their wiues
Roomes before hand: and oft it hits,
Not farre from them some Fish-wife sits.
For (here) of manners none take heed,
First come, first serd'd first serv'd, first feed.
Citizens, Souldiers, Sea-men, Schollers,
Gentlemen, Clownes, Millers, Colliers,
Mercers, Taylors, Poets, Booke-bynders,
Grocers, Curriers, Goldsmiths, goldfiners,
Silkemen, Botchets, Drapers, Dray-men,
Courtiers, Carters, Church-men, Lay-men,
Midwiues, Apple-wiues, Cheape-side Ladies,
Old Beldames, and yong Tiffany Babies,
Scotch-bums, red Wast-coats, fine Pawne-wenches,
         D   In

Pimlyco.

In the same roomes, on selfe same benches,
Crown'd All together: All Drincke, All Pay,
Why then should any giue the way?
Roomes here are by Reuersion got,
As Offices, so men win the Pot.
Both Pray and Pay, and wait, and woe,
That Foure may buy, what goes for two,
Yet tis refusde. The Serton scornes
To budge to a Knight. All stay their Tournes
As at the Conduit or the Mill,
And nothing's heard, but Fill, Fill, Fill,
Bespeaking one anothers Cups.
As men do Chayres in Barbors shops
On Christmasse Ceues. A hundred laps
Yeld vp for cakes; As many caps
Put off for Ale, whose iuice embalmes
Their Browes) tis beg'd as t'were an almes,
Yet all hold Siluer vp, and cry
Take mine, (as at the Lottery.)
  Drawers need not baule Anon, Anon,
Each Guest for his owne Drinck does run,
Braue men turne Tapsters, Women Caters,
For Ten that sit, there s Forty Waiters,
French-Hoods, and Veluet Caps being prowd
Sometimes, i'th Henroost close to crowd.
  O strange! what makes the Cripple heere:
When strongest legs can hardly beare
Those that stand on them, if they stand
But stiffly tw't in Pimlyco Land:
Yet euen that Wretch, (that halts on wood)
Althoe fiue farlongs off it stood,
Sweares hee's lympe tw't, and tw't hee goes,
And being there, his false legs does lose.
After him, gropes the Blind, and cries,
Pimlyco drincks not ont mine Eyes.
Pimlyco does so please the Mouth,
They come from East, West, North, & South.
  O Thou, (the Pimlyconian Host,)

                                        Had

Pimlyco.

Had thy Head bin but like that Post,
Which Scores what Ale and Cakes come in,
Of greater Reckoning hadſt thou bin.
Hadſt thou had Braines, but like to ſome,
To know what Wether was to come
By'th Almanacke ; thou hadſt changde thy lucke,
Thy Hynde ere this had proou'de a Bucke.
Alacke ! thy wits are loſt in Brewings;
Th'art growne ſtarke mad with too good Doings
Thou, onely cryeſt, Who payes the Shot?
(When the Maine Matters are forgot.)
Thou Barny Foole, at laſt grow wiſe,
Build thy Houſe round with Galleries,
Like to a Play-houſe ; for thy Ale
(Bæ't bad, bæ't good, bæt new, bæ't Stale)
Brings thæ good Audience : from each ſhore,
Ships of Fooles lanch, to ſæke thy Dore;
Ere prodigall Gulls ſaile backe agen,
Thei'le pay thæ money to come in:
Keepe then, thy wife and thou, the dores,
Let thoſe within wipe out the Scores.
Yet (O bile counſell!) why do I labour
To haue a Chriſtian wrong his neighbour?
Each afternoone thy Houſe being full,
Makes Fortune blind, or Gelds The Bull.
No, no, (thou Pimlyconian Brewer)
Thy Caſtle of Comfort ſtands ſo ſure,
(Moated with Ale, and wal'd with cakes)
Tho whirle-winds blow, it neuer ſhakes;
Therefore it næds no reparations,
No Rampyres, no Fortifications,
But onely Shot : Charge them Pell Mell,
Let Pimlyco Ordinance go off well;
And Hogſdon ſæmes a Towne of warre,
Where Conſtables the Captaines are,
Leading to Stocks (with Bils and Staues)
Whole trœpes of druncken Whores and Knaues,
Who (tho they cannot ſtand) yet go,

Pimlyco.

Swearing, Zounds hey braue Pimlyco.

   You therefore that do trade in Cans,
(Virginians, or Cracouians,)
You that in whole pots drinke your bone,
Lying dead-druncke at The Labor in vaine:
You Apron men, that weekely get
By your hard labour and your sweat,
Siluer (earn'd deare, but honestly)
Enough to find your family,
Now leaue those places (nam'd before)
Or if you'le Drinke, maintaine a Score,
But let your Wages (in one Summe)
Be wisely sau'd till Sunday come,
But (with it) buy, nor bread, nor broth,
Nor house, nor hose, nor shoe, nor cloth,
For food let wife and children Die,
Sucke Pimlyco downe merrily,
There dance and spend the day in laughter,
T'is meat and drinke a whole weeke after.

   You Ballad-Singers, that doe liue
On halfe penny almes that Ideots giue,
In euery Street (to druncken Sotes)
Set out your villanous yelping throates,
That through all eares your Tunes may flow,
With praises of Browne Pimlyco.

   You Poets that of Helicon boast,
Whose mornings drought without a toast
You alwayes take, but ne're do so,
Comming to tipple Pimlyco,)
O be more wise, and scorne that licquor,
Drincke this, which makes your Muses quicker,
Of This, three full Pots (I assure yee)
Leaues you starke drunke with brauer furie.

   You that plough up the salt Sea flood,
To fetch from farre, the Grapes deare blood.
And with Out-landish drinks confound
And mad the Brayne that is most sound:
Your very Ships going neuer so steddy,

                          (With

Pimlyco.

(With that moist Freight) but euer giddy
And ræling (as an ominous Signe,
That Those must ræle, who Trade in Wine,
From Shoze to Shoze what næd you faile,
When Pimlyco bzæds such Dzagon-flee?

  You that of men dære recknings make,
Yet at the Barre(for what they Take)
Arraigne them, Charging them to Stand,
Till they haue all held vp The Hand:
Downe with your Bushes, and your Grates,
Dzaw your selues thozow the Citie Gates,
To Sacke the Walls of Pimlyco,
Which day by day moze strong do grow,
And will in time (to their owne Trench)
Dzine backe both Spanish Wines and French:
Oz if no Shot can batter downe
This Pimlyco Fort ; then, in the Towne,
And in the fields and Common way,
Pitch Tents, and openly display
Your Banners (dzawne with Red and White)
Vnder those cullozs Men will fight
Till they can stand, else All are lost,
And cut off by the Pimlyco Host,
Here therefoze sownd, Anon, Anon,
Foz the mayne Army here coms on.

  O you that (euery Mone) hold Feasts,
(And in the True-loue-knot are Guests)
And doe with Wreathes your Temples crowne,
(At Lothbury, and at Horsey-downe,)
Let those Deare Fleshly-Meetings go,
And Bath your Bzaynes in Pimlyco.

  You that by Enginous Whæles can fozce
Tydes to run backe and turne their Course,
Whose wits in water still do Diue,
(O, if you with that Trades should thzine,)
With lowd voyce to the Citie speake,
That she her Conduit-Heads would bzeake,
And onely build One Conduite-Head.

Pimlyco.

At Pimlyco, that through pipes of Lead,
The pretious Streame may be conuayd,
And Crafts-men so at home be stayd.

  You Bawds, yon Pandars, Puncks and whores,
That are chalk'd vp on Ale-house scores,
You that lay Petticoats, Gownes, and Smocks
To pawne for drincks to cure the Pore,
At Pimlyco some will take them from you,
To drinke there then, shall best become you.

  Of Aley-Ilands there are moe,
(Some new discouered, some before)
But neither th'Old nor New of name,
Can equall Pimlyco in fame.

  Of these strange Ilands, Malta is one,
Malta does Border close vpon
The Continent of Pimlyco,
And by her Streames more rich does grow,
On Pimlyco Seas when tis fowle weather,
That no Ship can get in; then hither,
(To Malta) flie they with swolne Saile,
To buy the Iew of Malta's Ale.
Thy Knights (O Malta) now do flourish,
Pimlyco their renowne does nourish,
All fealty therefore they doowe
And Seruice to guard Pimlyco.

  Tripoly from the Turke was taken,
But Tripoly is againe forsaken;
What Newes from Tripoly? Would you know?
Christians flye thence to Pimlyco.

  Eye-bright, (so'fam'd of late for Beere)
Although thy Name be numbred heere,
Thine ancient Honors now runne low;
Thou art struck blind by Pimlyco.
The New-found Land, is now growen stale,
Few to Terceras Ilands sayle;
The once well-mand, braue Ship of Hull,
That spred a sayle, proud, stiffe, and full,
Leakes oft, and does at Anchor lye :

                        Nay,

Pimlyco.

Nay, euen St. Christopher walkes dry.
Not halfe so many Christians (now)
Their knees before his White-crosse bow.
　Run, (Red-cap) Run, amongst the Rest,
Thou art nam'd last, that once wert best,
But (Red-cap) now thy Woll is worne,
By Pimlyco is Red-cap shorne.
　Our weary Muse (here) leapes to Shore,
On these rough Seas she Sayles no more,
This Voyage made she (for your sakes,)
Spending thus much in Ale and Cakes.

FINIS.

ANTIENT DROLLERIES.

(No. 1.)

Cobbes Prophecies,

1614.

REPRODUCED IN FACSIMILE BY

CHARLES PRAETORIUS,

WITH A PREFACE BY

A. H. BULLEN.

LONDON:
PRINTED FOR PRIVATE CIRCULATION.
1890.

ANTIENT DROLLERIES.

(NO. I.)

ANTIENT DROLLERIES.

(No. I.)

Cobbes Prophecies,

HIS SIGNES AND TOKENS, HIS MADRIGALLS,
QUESTIONS, AND ANSWERES, WITH HIS
SPIRITUALL LESSON, IN VERSE, RIME,
AND PROSE.

1614.

REPRODUCED IN FACSIMILE

BY

CHARLES PRAETORIUS,

WITH A PREFACE

BY

A. H. BULLEN.

LONDON:
PRINTED FOR PRIVATE CIRCULATION.
1890.

PREFACE.

JOHN DUNTON warned the readers of the *Rare Adventures of Don Kainophilus* that they would find the narrative " such a hodgpotch of stuff as would make a hermit tear his beard to hear of it." The description is not inapplicable to the drolling prophecies of Master Cobbe.

The preface is signed " Richard Rablet," who is evidently a fictitious personage. Mr. Bertram Dobell plausibly suggests that the author styled himself " Rablet " after François Rabelais, whose *Pantagrueline Prognostication* is familiar to everybody. It was not uncommon to issue these mock prognostications under assumed names. For instance, *Friar Bakons Prophesie*, published ten years before *Cobbes Prophecies*, purports to be by " William Terilo." *The Owles Almanacke*, 1618 (attributed without evidence to Dekker), bears on the title-page the name of " Mr. Jocundary Merrie-braines."

A mild Shakespearean interest attaches to *Cobbes Prophecies* from the resemblance that some of the

pieces bear to the Fool's prophecy in *Lear* (III. 2);
but the whimsical madrigals that follow the prophecies
are the salt of our curious tract. The verses on the
morrice-dance give a lively description of that old
English merriment; they should be compared with
the madrigal, in Thomas Morley's collection of 1594,
beginning—"Ho! who comes there with bagpiping
and drumming?" Richard Rablet was no puritan;
he loved

> " a pot of good Ale
> And a merry old tale."

By the fire-side among his cronies in winter,

> " When a Cup of good Sacke,
> That hurts not the backe,
>   will make the cheeks red as a Cherry,"

he would be ready with his jests and quips; and we
may be sure that in summer-time he was a welcome
guest at shearing-feasts and harvest-homes. His talk
is occasionally somewhat free, but doubtless he was
regarded as a privileged person. Besides, he has
stores of admirable counsel. How delicately he warns
impulsive maids to be chary of their favours at the
feast of St. Valentine!—

> " When the Grasse doth spring,
> And the Birds gin to sing,
>   take heed of St. Valentines day ;
> Least while ye reioyce,
> In lighting on your choyce,
>   ye make not ill worke before May."

Honest mirth is what he advocated. Time, that
blunts the lion's paws, will too soon dull the briskness
of our lustiest springals. So let the younkers frisk it
while they may. "Nunc levis est tractanda Venus,"
as gentle Tibullus urges. Does not Ovid remind us
(though, sooth to say, the reminder is hardly needed)
that crookt age comes with noiseless step, "Jam veniet
tacito curva senecta pede"? Our cheerful moralist
prescribes for old and young—

> "When a man is old,
> And the wether blowes cold,
>   well fare a fire and a fur'd Gowne :
> But when he is young,
> And his blood new sprung,
>   his sweete hart is worth half the Towne.
>
> When a Maid is faire,
> In her smocke and haire,
>   who would not be glad to woe her ? "

A graver note is struck in the poem, "When
Youth and Beauty meet togither"; and "Cobs talke
with Wisedome" affords matter for serious reflection.
But, take it all in all, the book is mere drollery; a
tale of a roasted horse, a riot of mad rhymes, a
pleasant piece of tomfoolery.

1, *Yelverton Villas, Twickenham,*
   25th June, 1890.

COBBES PROPHECIES, HIS SIGNES AND TOKENS,

his Madrigalls, Queſtions, and An-
ſweres, with his ſpirituall Leſſon, in
Verſe, Rime, and Proſe.

Pleaſant, and not vnprofitable.

Reade that will, Iudge that can, Like
that liſt.

Printed at London for *Robert Wilſon*, and are to be ſold
at his Shop at Grayes-Inne Gate.
1 6 1 4.

To the Reader.

THere was vpon a time an odde Country Riming Fellow, whoſe name was Cobbe: where hee dwelt, I finde not ; and what hee was, it skils not: Onely this I note of him, that it ſeemes by the Memoriall I haue of him, that he was in his time, as (no doubt are many now adaies) giuen to looke ſo farre aboue the Moone, that as falling through the Clouds, when he wak t, he knew not where he was: but ſtrange thinges he had in his head, which he ſet downe as oddely in writing : where if you looke for verſe, you are out ; if for Rime, you are in : now, if you take delight in old idle Prophecies, ſtrange Signes and Tokens, though they neuer come to paſſe, and to reade now and than of many a ſtrange Madrigall, heere you may haue change to fit your choiſe; how they will fall fit with your humour I know not, and therefore this is all I will ſay to you. I know

the

To the Reader.

*the Book Seller will ſay. What lack you, and I ſay,
I wiſh all may like you ; ſo, till I ſee you, though I
know you not when I meete you, to the Lord of heauen I leaue you.*

Your well willer as to all

honeſt Men.

Richard Rablet.

COBBES PROPHECIES,
HIS MADRIGALS, SIGNES,
AND TOKENS.

Hen fashions make mens Bodies,
And wits are rul'd by Noddies :
When Fooles grow rich by fortune,
And wise must fooles importune.
When Greyhounds must cry crauen,
And Mastiue Dogges must rauen :
When Faulcons stoope to carren,
And Poulcats spoile the warren.
The Sunne doth leaue his shining,
The Moone is in declining :
The Starres are ouer-shrouded,
The Sky is ouer clouded.
The Ayre is all infected,
The Plague yet not respected :
No Charity nor pitty,
In Country, nor in Citty.
The vertuous all disgraced,
The famous all defaced :
And rascall kinde of people,
Shall looke aboue Paules steeple :
When Nightingales are scorned,
And Cuckoes are adorned.
And Black-birds leaue their whistle,
And pearch vpon a Thistle :
And Oates are sowne and gathered,
And Children are strange fathered.

And

Prophecies.

And Swannes do loose their feathers,
While Geese fortell foule weathers:
When Horses tug at Cables,
While Asses keepe the Stables.
When Virgins waite on whoores,
And Knights keepe Beggars doores :
And Iackes like Knights shall Iet it,
Because their purses get it,
When Noble-minded Spirits,
Can haue no hope of Merits;
But either quite discarded,
Or slenderly rewarded :
When Owles, and Apes, and Asses,
Shall pranke themselues in Glasses.
While better kind of Creatures,
Of farre more dainty Natures,
Shall clad in cloath of lether,
To hold out winde and wether.
When Schollars mocke their Teachers,
And Lay men laugh at Preachers :
And woodcockes learne of wizards,
To play the doting dizards.
When foule flaps shall be painted,
And faire paps shall bee tainted,
And patience must content her,
That no man will lament her :
But all things topsie-turuy,
Do proue the world so scuruy,
That honest men abhorre it,
Why ? then, who will care for it ?
But, that no such ill season,
Where truth may dye by treason.

The

The wicked foole may flourish,
While none the good will nourish :
Or Earth be feene or heard,
To make the world afeard :
Pray all good hearts with me,
That it may neuer be.

WHen lacke of grace turnes good to euill,
And men leaue God to ferue the Deuill :
And young men follow imperfections,
And old men dote in ill affections.
When Beauty is a baite of finning,
While wanton threds, make wicked fpinning,
And wealth doth onely breede ambition,
When Nature fhewes an ill condition.
And bafeneffe buyes the Badge of Honor,
VVhile VVifedome weepes to looke vpon her;
VVhen learning teacheth but illufion,
VVhere fancies ftudy but confufion.
When power is feene but in oppreffion,
VVhile confcience makes no finnes confeffion :
VVhen Lechery is Natures follace,
And Robbery is Reafons purchace.
VVhen peace doth breede an ill fecurity,
Where pleafure liues but in impurity :
When fimple vertue is difdained,
And fubtill vice is entertained :
If fuch a time fhould euer be,
That, I hope, neuer man fhall fee.
That fo the wicked fiende fhould rage,
In euery courfe of euery age;

B   That

That lack of Grace should thinke it good,
To liue vpon the fruit of blood;
While Spirits carelesse of saluation,
Will headlong runne vnto damnation:
Pray to the Lord of heauen to mend it,
Or in his mercy, quickly end it.

WHen Tradesmen take no Mony,
   Nor Varmin hunt a Cony:
Old Mumpsie is no Meacocke,
Nor his proud Minckes a Peacocke.
The Souldiour is not bloody,
His Ostesse is not muddy;
The Vsurer not greedy,
The rich releeue the needy:
The Courtier is not haughty,
His Courtizan not naughty.
The wantons leaue their winking,
The damned crew their drinking:
The Geese do leaue their grazing,
And idle eies their gazing:
Dame Parnell is no pratler,
Her parasite no flatterer:
The Chapmen leaue their buying
And Sellers leaue their lying.
The Skipper leaues his sayling,
The Oyster-wiues their rayling;
The Farmer leaues his tillage,
The Begger leaues the village.
When Snudges leaue their sparing.
And Coseners leaue their sharing:

When

When Theeues doe leaue their robbing,
And heauy harts their throbbing:
When proud men leaue their spighting,
And Poets leaue their byting:
When Children leaue their crying,
And old men leaue their dying;
Strange will be the alteration,
Or elfe, a confummation.

VVHen Ships doe faile againſt the winde,
   And Nature goes againſt her kinde :
And tongues muſt fay that blacke is white,
While mad men make a day of night :
When Reafon muſt fubfcribe to will,
To leaue the good and take the ill.
When Confcience fits and blowes the cole,
While Patience liues on pitties dole:
And Wifedome fhall be poore and bare,
While folly lights on Fortunes fhare;
And learning doth but breake the braine,
While bare Experience gets the gaine:
And loue is plaid on follies Stage,
Twixt Youth, and Ages marriage.
And Auarice with ielous eies,
Doth liue in greefe, while pleafure dies :
And man becomes but Monies Slaue,
While Vertue liues in Honors Graue;
When Nature thus doth change her courfe,
From good to bad, from ill to worfe.
And, hope of mendment will be fmall,
When thus the Deuill workes in all:

If

Prophecies.

If euer man should liue to know
The wailefull time of so much woe:
As God forbid should euer be,
That Eare should heare, or Eye should see:
Then harty prayers would do well,
For sauing of the Soule from Hell.

VVHen the Fisherman drownes the Eele,
And the Hare bites the Huntsman by the heel:
When the Geese do driue the Foxe into his hole,
And the Thistle ouertops the May-pole.
The Hering is at warre with the Whale,
And the Drunkard forsweares a pot of Ale:
When the Lawyers plead all for pitty,
And conscience is the Ruler of a Citty;
When the parson will his Tithes forgoe,
And the Parish will pay him, will, or no.
When the Vsurer is weary of his gaine,
And the Farmer feedes the poore with his graine:
The Oyster leaues gaping for the tide,
And Lob Iolly will not daunce with his Bride.
When Prentizes had rather worke then play,
And Schollars cannot away with a holy-day:
When brabbles and quarrels all cease,
And Armies yeelde their Armies to peace;
And peace such a power hath won,
That Souldiers serue all with a Potgun.
When the Fletcher fals out with the Bolt,
And the wife must make cursie to a Dolt,
When the Night is brighter then the Day,
And the Cloudes driue the winde away.

When

Prophecies.

When the Snow and the Froſt are fire hot,
And the Coſtermongers Apples will not rot:
When the Aſſe ſhall make Muſique to the Owle,
And the Slut will not weare her cloaths foule.
When the Ship ſhall throw away her ſaile,
And the Dogge ſhall leaue wagging of his taile;
And the Rabbets ſhall runne through the Hey,
And the Varmin makes the Warriner runne away:
When the Cat is afraid of the Mouſe,
And the Beggar will walke without a Louſe.
When Connies doe Caſtles vndermine,
And Lords muſt waite while Lobcockes dine:
And rich men weepe, and Beggars ſing,
And euery Knaue will be a King.
Vntill the Gallowes, or the Whip,
Doe take a Villaine in a Trip:
When all things thus doe come to paſſe,
That by an Oxe, and by an Aſſe;
The queſtion ſhall decided be,
Why Dogges and Cats cannot agree.
When Mowles and Wormes do looke abroad,
And Snakes doe combat with the Toade:
The Fleyes will not abide the ſheetes,
Nor idle people walke the ſtreetes,
When thus the world doth come about
Within the courſe of *Colin Clout*:
Which neuer man I hope ſhall ſee,
God knowes what then the world will be.

WHen the Winter to Summer turneth,
   The Fire cooles, and the water burneth;

When

Prophecies.

When the Fly puts the Eagle to her flight,
And the day holds a Candle to the night:
When the trees bend downe to the bushes,
And the Owle driues the Nightingale to hushes:
When the Hare fals to play with the Hound,
And the Worme scornes to creepe into the ground;
When the Aspe with the Wolfe makes a fray,
And the Mouse makes the Cat runne away.
When the Owle teacheth the Parrat to speake,
And the Goose makes the Gander to keake:
When the Market Crosse is without Corne,
And not a house will yeeld a man a horne.
When the Clouds commaund the winde to be still,
And the Valley will ouertop the hill:
When the Storke is afraid of the Frog,
And the Cur runs away from the Hog.
When the Beggars will leaue the high way,
And wantons will giue ouer play;
When a Moris-dance is without a foole,
And a foole be without a Ladle and a toole:
When rich wares will be at low rate,
And a Citty will runne out at the Gate:
The Sailer cannot away with a merry gale,
And the Constable is afraid of a pot of Ale.
When the Goose is mistaken for the Swan,
And the Goodwife knowes not her good Man;
If the world were come to such a change,
The alteration would be very strange:
But rather then all should go so amisse,
Better be content with it, as it is.

When

Prophecies.

VVHen the day and the night do meete,
   And the houſes are euen with the ſtreete :
And the fire and the water agree,
And blinde men haue power to ſee :
When the Wolfe and the Lambe liue togither,
And the blaſted trees will not wither.
When the flood and the ebbe runne one way,
And the Sunne and the Moone are at a ſtay ;
When Age and Youth are all one,
And the Miller creepes through the Mill-ſtone :
When the Ram butts the Butcher on the head,
And the liuing are buried with the dead.
VVhen the Cobler doth worke without his eends,
And the Cutpurſe, and the Hangman are friends :
Strange things will then be to ſee,
But I thinke it will neuer be.

VVHen the wind is alwaies in one place,
   All Horſes are of one Race :
And all Men are in one caſe.

When all words haue but one ſence,
All Caſes are in one tence ;
And all Purſes haue but one expence.

VVhen all hands do ſit one Gloue,
All harts haue but one Loue :
And all Birds be but one Doue.

VVhen all wit is in one head,
And all Corne makes but one bread ;
And all eaſe is in one bed.

VVhen

Prophecies.

When all Truth is in one hart,
And all Knowledge is in one art,
And all Diuisions are in one part.

When all sport is in one play,
When all feasts are in one day:
And all States are at one stay.

When all faces haue but one feature,
And all Spirits are of one Nature;
And all worth is in one Creature.

Such wonders will be then to see,
As out of doubt will neuer be.

WHen there is nothing but sorrow and care,
And the fieldes are all barren and bare;
And the Beggers haue a miserable share.

When the Markets are horrible deere,
There is nothing to drinke, but small beere :
And the rich men keepe beggerly cheere.

When the Children are bawling and crying,
And old folkes are swearing and lying :
And sicke folkes are sighing and dying.

When Baiard is downe in the mire,
And the fat is all in the fire :
When loue hath lost his desire.

When Maisters do fall into rages,

And

And Seruants are vnpaid their wages ;
And all their best clothes are in gages.

If euer it should come about,
To put the Cockes eies cleane out :
And then hope to reuell and rout.

Which I hope neuer to see,
But where all faire Gamsters be ;
Good fellowes will kindly agree.

God knowes, for I cannot tell,
Who then goes to Heauen or to Hell.

VVHen Preachers haue louing Auditors,
    And Borrowers haue kind Creditors :
When Sutors petitions haue comfortable reading,
And *Forma pauperis* hath a fauourable pleading.
VVhen loue is the whole rule of life,
And the Good man loues none but his owne wife,
VVhen there is no spleene, nor any spight,
But euery one keepes his owne right :
VVhen all is as plaine as the high-way,
And all goes by yea, and by nay.
And one man so well loues another,
That there is no false Sister nor Brother,
No facing, frowning, nor fighting,
But one in another delighting ;
No oddes twixt the Groome and the Bride,
No enuy, nor mallice, nor pride.
No punishment, but for offences,

C   No

No care, but all for expences.
No time spent, but all businesse,
Nor sleeping, but all in heauinesse:
No iarring, but all in iesting,
No friendship, but all in feasting.
No lawing, brabling, nor bribing,
No kind of scoffing, nor gibing;
No painting of ill fauored faces,
Nor seeking of true loues disgraces :
No tale, but well worth the telling,
Nor fauour, but well worth the smelling.
No Act, but well worth the doing,
No Wench, but well worth the woing;
If such a time were happily come,
To proue this true in all, or some;
Who would not ioy in hart to see,
And pray it might so euer be.

WHen toies and trifles stand for treasure,
    And pain mistaken stands for pleasure:
When lust mistaken is for loue,
A Iack-daw for a Turtle-doue.
When Craft is taine for Honesty,
Hypocrisie, for Piety ;
And babling held for eloquence,
And basenesse stands for excellence:
When truth shall be esteem'd a iest,
And he thats rich, is onely blest.
While all the vertues of the mind,
Do all go whirling downe the wind.
And braine spun thred shall be esteemd,
And Wisedome little worth be deemd:

And

And flatterers fhail ftand for friends,
To bring but fooles to idle ends :
When nothing fhall be well begun,
But croft, or fpoild ere it be done.
And euery where the bad for good,
Shall be too much mifvnderftood ;
While wilfull folly fhould reioyce,
In making of a wicked choyce :
And true difcretion grieue to fee,
In what a cafe the curfed be
If fuch a time was neuer fuch,
Should come to curffe the world fo much:
As God forbid it fhould be fo,
That Man fhould fo much forrow know ;
That Deuils fo fhould play their parts,
Then vp to Heauen with honeft harts.

WHen feuen Geefe follow one Swan,
And feuen Cats licke in one pan :
When feuen Iack-dawes follow one Crow,
And feuen Archers fhoot in one Bow.
When feuen Citties make but one State,
And feuen houfes haue but one Gate :
When feuen Armies make but one Campe,
And feuen States haue but one ftamp :
When feuen Schollers haue but one gown,
And feuen Lordfhips, make but one towne.
When feuen Swagrers haue but one Punck,
And feuen trauallers haue but one truncke.
When feuen Horfes faddle one Mare,
And feuen Pedlers haue but one packe of ware :

C 2

When

Prophecies.

When seuen Hackney Men haue but one Iade,
And seuen Cutlers haue but one Blade;
When seuen Butcl rs haue but one staule,
And seuen Coblers, haue but one aule:
When seuen riuers haue but one Fish,
And seu:n Tables haue but one Dish.
When seuen Lawyers plead but one case,
And seuen Painters worke vpon one face:
When seuen Ditties haue but one Note,
And seuen Fidlers haue but one Grote.
When seuen Guls haue but one throat,
And seuen Truls, haue but one peticoat;
If by the number thus of seuen,
The one doe make the odde full euen:
That, in the sence of the conceit,
The seuen to one doe make vp eight.
It seemes not strange yet vnto me
Tis strange, now ecuen and odde agree:
Yet when it fals, tis no deceit,
That seuen and one doe make vp eight.

VVHen the Hen crowes,
  Then the Cocke knowes
    what worke must be done,
And when the wind blowes,
Then the Sailer knowes
    what course must be runne.

When the Mill goes,
Then the Miller knowes
    what Fish are a flote:

                                                find

Madrigals.

And when the tide flowes,
Then the Water-man knowes,
   what to doe with his Boate.

When the Graffe growes.
Then the Mower knowes,
   what to do with his Sithe :
And when the Farmer fowes,
Then the Parfon knowes
   he fhall haue a Tithe.

When the Buckes take the Does,
Then the Warriner knowes,
   there are Rabbets in breeding:
And when the Bag fhowes,
Then the Milke maid knowes
   the Cow hath good feeding.

WHen the day peepeth,
   And the Husbandman fleepeth,
   he loofeth the gaine of the morning,
But when the Ducke quaketh,
And *Sim* his *Sufan* waketh,
   take heed of working for horning.

When the Bell ringeth,
And Robin-redbreft fingeth,
   vp maids and make cleane your Dairy;
Bnt if ye lye and ftretch ye,
Vntill the lazy catch ye,
   take heed that ye meete not the Fairy.
When

Madrigals.

When the Cow loweth,
And Cocke-a-doodle croweth,
   vp maids and put on your raiment:
For if ye keepe your beds
Till ye loose your maiden heads,
   take heed of a forty weeks paiment.

But when the Starre shooteth,
And the Owle hooteth,
   to bed then and take your ease :
But when ye would rest,
Take heed in your nest,
   ye find not worse varmin then fleas.

When the Dogge howleth,
And your Dame scowleth,
   then wenches take heed of foule weather:
But when the Mouse peepeth,
And your Dame sleepeth,
   then laugh and be merry togither.

When the Watch walketh,
And at the doore talketh,
   Lads and Guirles, looke to your doores;
Then to bed roundly,
And sleepe there as soundly,
   as if ye were all knaues and whores.

WHen a man is old,
   And the wether blowes cold,
   well fare a fire and a fur'd Gowne :

But

But when he is young,
And his blood new fprung,
   his fweete hart is worth halfe the Towne.

When a Maid is faire,
In her fmocke and haire,
   who would not be glad to woe her:
But when fhe goes to bed,
To loofe her maiden-head,
   how kindly her Good-man goes to her

When the Graffe doth fpring,
And the Birds gin to fing,
   take heed of St. Valentines day;
Leaft while ye reioyce,
In lighting on your choyce,
   ye make not ill worke before May.

When the Sunnes fhines bright,
And the Day is light,
   then Shepheards abroad with your flocks:
But if the Heyfer play,
And the Heard be away,
   take heed the Bull prooue not an Oxe.

When the Corne is ripe,
And the Straw makes a pipe,
   then to it with the Sithe and the Sickle.
But when ye make the ftacke,
If ye lye on your backe,
   take heed how ye laugh till ye tickle.

Madrigals.

When the Apples fall,
And the Patridges call,
    Then Farmers haue home with your Corne
Bnt when ye make your Mowes,
Take heed to your Cowes,
    they beare not a sheafe on a horne.

When the trees doe bud,
And the Kids chew the cud,
    then fall to your digging and sowing:
But if your seede be nought,
Or your worke be ill wrought;
    then blame not the ground for ill growing.

When the Sunne is downe,
And the Guests come to towne,
    long trauailers lightly are weary.
But if mine Oste be a good fellow,
And mine Ostesse be not yellow;
    who then would not laugh and be merry.

IN the month of May,
Is a pretty play,
    is called youths wooing;
But long it will not last,
For when that May is past,
    there will be no doing.

For loue is so quicke,
He stands on a pricke,
    that likes no delaying:

Madrigals.

For idle excufes,
Are but loues abufes,
    that marre all the Maying.

The fquint of an eye,
May oft looke awry,
    in fancies new fafhion :
But winke and fhake the head,
And the colour once dead,
    there is the true paffion.

When the eye reedeth,
How the hart bleedeth,
    in filence true teares :
Then eafily may the mind,
If that it be not blind,
    fee what the fpirit beares.

For paffions ftaid lookes,
Are Truths only books,
    where kindneffe beft reedeth ;
The time and the place,
In beauties beft grace,
    how loue euer fpeedeth.

VVHen the time of the yeare,
    Doth cal for good cheere,
  why fhould we not laugh and be merry;
When a Cup of good Sacke,
That hurts not the backe,
  will make the cheeks red as a Cherry.

             D   VVhen

Madrigals.

When the thred is all spun,
And the worke is all done,
    why should not the work-folkes go play:
When a pot of good Ale,
And a merry old tale,
    would passe the time smoothly away.

When the Medowes are growne,
And the Grasse abroad throwne,
    for shame giue the wench a green gowne;
But when the Harueft is in,
And the Bread in the Bin,
    then, Piper play laugh and lye downe.

When my Dame fals to Bake
A Pudding and a Cake,
    will make cheare in Bowles;
But when the Oyle of Malt,
Makes the heeles for to halt,
    take heed of your lop heauy Nowles.

IN the olde time,
When an odde-pumpe rime,
    would haue made a Dog laugh :
And the Osteffe of the Swan,
Would swinge her good Man,
    with a good quarter ftaffe.

When more then a good many,
Had nine Egges a penny,
    and Corne was sixe pence a strike;

                                      Then

Then true blinde deuotion,
Brought such to promotion,
    As neuer I hope will be like.

When the Cat kild the Mouse,
And the Dog kept the house,
    and all was wholesome and cleanely;
And *Iohn* and his *Ioane*,
Did liue of their owne,
    full merily, though but all meanely.

When Beefe, Bread and Beere,
Was honest mens cheere,
    and welcome and spare not :
And the Man kist the Maid,
And was not affraid,
    come who will I care not.

When right should haue reason,
In time, place and season,
    and Truth was beleeued;
When these things did go thus,
Which Truth doth not show vs,
    then Charity flourisht :
When loue and good Nature
In euery Creature,
    a kind Spirit nourisht.

But if that it were so,
As many do feare no,
    that some were sore blinded;

                    What

What euer the caufe was,
Tis now at another paffe,
   men are otherwife minded.

For fuch as haue prooued,
What is to beloued,
   will euer be heedfull :
That nothing be wanting,
Though fomewhat be fcanting,
   to comfort the needfull.

And therefore no matter,
How ere fooles do flatter,
   their wits with their will;
I wifh the time prefent,
In all true contentment,
   to ftay with vs ftill.

IF the day were as long as the yeare,
  And the Goffips were making good cheere,
   they would thinke the time were but fhort :
But if they fall to brawling and fcolding,
And the Beggars be at the vpholding,
   oh there would be delicate fport.

If the Apples were once in the fire,
Each Goffip had her pot by her,
   and euery one to her tale :
And the Wife that went once for a maid,
Would tell what trickes fhe had plaid,
   oh there would be worke for whole fale.

If the Wine once did worke in the braine,
And the Wenches were right in the vaine,
   then talke of the reckoning to morrow;
Let Husbands take care for their wiues,
And Goſſips make much of their liues,
   they are fooles that will dye for ſorrow.

IT was my hap of late by chance,
     oh pretty chance;
To meet a Country Moris-dance,
     oh pretty dance.
When cheefeſt of them all the foole,
     oh pretty foole :
Plaied with a Ladle and a toole,
     oh pretty toole :
When euery Younker ſhak't his Bels,
     oh pretty Bels ;
Till ſweating feete, gaue fohing ſmels,
     oh fohing ſmels.
And fine Maide-Marian with her ſmoile,
     oh pretty ſmoile :
Shew'd how a Raſcall plaid the Roile,
     oh pretty Roile.
But when the Hobby-horſe did wihy,
     oh pretty wihy ;
Then all the Wenches gaue a tihy,
     oh pretty tihy.
But when they gan to ſhake their Boxe,
     oh pretty Boxe :
And not a Gooſe could catch a Foxe,
     oh pretty Foxe.

                The

Signes and Tokens.

The Piper then put vp his pipes,
      oh pretty pipes ;
And allthe Woodcoks lookt like Snipes,
      oh pretty Snipes.
And therewith fell a showry streame,
      oh pretty streame :
That I awakt out of my dreame,
      oh scuruy dreame.

Signes and Tokens.

VVHen Charing-Crosse and Pauls Church meet,
    And breake their fast in Friday street :
When Ware and Waltham goe to Kent
Togither, there to purchase Rent.
When Islington and Lambeth ioyne,
To make a voyage to the Groine :
And Southwarke with St. Katherines gree,
To ride in post to Couentry :
When Turmcle-street and Clarken-well,
Haue sent all Bawdes and Whores to Hell :
And Long-ditch, and Long-laue do try,
Antiquities for honesty ;
And Newgate weepes, and Bridewell greeues,
For want of Beggars, Whores, and Theeues.
And Tyburne doth to Wapping sweare,
Shall neuer more come Hang-man there :
When blinde men see, and dumbe men read,
Which seemes impossible indeed.
And by all rules that I can see,
I thinke in truth will neuer be.

                             Then

Then, then ye may fay then,
Knaues now will be honeſt men.

VV Hen Youth and Beauty meet togither,
     theres worke for Breath ;
But when they both begin to wither,
     theres worke for Death.

When Loue and Honor worke togither,
     theres worke for Fame;
But when they both begin to wither,
     theres worke for ſhame.

When Hope and Labour go togither,
     theres worke for gaine,
But when they both begin to wither,
     theres worke for paine.

When Wit and Vertue worke togither,
     their work goes well;
But when they both begin to wither,
     theres worke for Hell.

Let then perfeƈtions liue togither,
     and worke for praiſe.
For when their worke begins to wither,
     their worth decaies.

IF all Rules of Phiſicke,
Had onely help for the Tiſicke;
And all Chirurgeries ground,
Were for the healing of one wound.

And all kind of preaching,
Were but for one Parish teaching,
And all kind of diet,
To keepe one tongue in quiet.
And all kind of pleasures,
Were but for one mans treasures;
And all kind of learning,
Were for one points discerning;
And all kind of disputing,
Were for one points confuting.
And all kind of writing,
Were for one mans delighting :
If there should be such a season,
All so to go against reason;
Which I thinke neuer to see,
Let them that know thinke what will be,

VVHen the Rich are all agreed,
    On the purses of the poore to feede:
And the wise men finde out fooles Lands,
To get them all into their hands.
And Wenches haue tricks with their eics,
To catch men, as Candles do Flies :
And Swagrers make the high-way,
The cheefest part of their stay.
When Bawds and Whores study the Art,
To scape the Whip and the Cart ;
And Cut-purses all take their oathes,
To keepe the Hang-man in cloathes.
When thus the Deuill doth lurke,
To fall with the world to his worke :
Which would be a great sorrow to see,
Pray, that it may neuer be.

Questi-

Qu. WHy should a rich man become a Theefe?
An. Becaufe the fweete of gaine ouercomes his (fence.
Que. Why should any man want Mony?
An. Becaufe fome fpend it fafter then they can get it.
Que. Why are old folkes in loue?
An. Becaufe eafe breeds idleneffe.
Que. Why is Tobacco in fuch efteeme?
An. Becaufe it dries vp Rheume, and fpends drinke.
Que. Why do fo many people vfe gaming?
An. Becaufe they want wit for better exercife
Que. Why is a Cuckold patient?
An. Becaufe of profit or feare.
Que. Why are men iealous of their wiues?
An. Becaufe they are Fooles.
Que. Why are offenders punifht?
An. To keepe the Subiects in peace.
Que. Why are Gallants flattered?
An. For a Fooles pride, and a Knaues profit.
Que. Why do Children cry?
An. Becaufe they know not what they would haue.
Que. Why doe Beggars skold?
An. Becaufe they are commonly drunke.
Que. Why doe Apes counterfeit men?
An. Becaufe men counterfeit Apes.
Que. Why are Lawes ordained?
An. To giue euery man his right.
Qu. Why are their fuch delaies in their execution?
An. Becaufe there are fo many caufes to difpatch.
Que. What makes wares deere in the world?
An. The multitude of people,

E

Que.

Qu. And what makes cheapnesse?
An. Aboundance.

Qu. Where is the best dwelling in the world?
An. In a mans owne house.

Qu. And where is the best being for all men?
An. In Heauen.

Qu. What is of most esteeme in the world?
An. Mony.

Qu. what is the least cared for of a great many?
An. Conscience.

Qu. Why is honesty with many held a Iest?
A. Because there are so few honest in earnest.

Qu. Which is the best ground to plant on?
An. That which is a mans owne.

Qu. why should Beggars liue without labour?
An. Because their Mony comes in easily.

Qu. Why do Gamsters fall out so oft?
An. Because losse breeds impatience.

Qu. why are rich men most sickly?
An. Because they take to much ease.

Qu. what is the best Phisicke for all Natures?
An. Motion.

Qu. When is best taking Phisicke?
An. When one is sicke.

Qu. What sicknesse is most dangerous?
An. The Plague.

Qu. What most vnsightly?
An. The Poxe.

Qu. What most continuing?
An. The Ague.

Qu. What most incurable?

An. The Gout.

Qu. What most painefull?

An. The Tooth-ach.

Qu. What most common?

An. The Rheume.

Qu. What is ill for the eye-sight?

An. An Enemy.

Qu. What is good for it?

An. Gold.

Qu. What is the fruit of Learning?

An. Pride, pleasure, or profit.

Qu. What is the honor of the Law?

An. Iustice.

Qu. What is the Glory of the Law?

An. Mercy.

Qu. And what is the force of the Law?

An. Obedience.

Qu. VVhat makes Lawyers rich?

An. Contentions of Clients.

Qu. What makes Magistrates honorable?

An. Execution of Iustice.

Qu. What is the poore mans happinesse?

An. Patience.

Qu. And what is the wise mans wealth

An. Content.

Qu. VVhy are faire women most loued?

An. Because mens eies marre their wits.

Qu. VVhy do wise men keepe Fooles?

An. To exercise their Charity.

Qu. VVhy are Diuines most worthy Reuerence?

An. Because they are the mouths of God vnto his

Qu. VVhy are so many Sects in Religion? (people.

An.

Questions and Answers.

An. Becaufe the Deuil fowes fedition in the Church.

Que. Why do many befoole themfelues with Idolatry?

A. Becaufe blindnes in deuotiõ breeds indifcretion.

Que. Why fhould wife men be vndone by furetifhip?

An. Becaufe their loue exceeds their wits.

Qu. Why are men vndone by women?

An. Becaufe they had rather be flaues then free-men.

Que. Why do many Louers grow franticke?

An. Becaufe they feek that which is hard to be found.

Que. Why do mad men talke fo much?

A. Becaufe their tongues wag with the wind of their

Que. Why are honeft harts moft croffed?   (braine.

An. To try their patience.

Qu. When are the patient moft happy?

An. At the houre of Death:

Que. What is the greateft feare in the world?

An. To dye.

Que. What is the greateft greefe?

An. Want.

Que. Why do Phifitions die?

An. Becaufe Death is to cunning for them.

Que. Why doe men cry out vpon Fortune?

An. To excufe their follies.

Que. Why do Labourers fing?

An. For the hope of their wages.

Que. Why do wife men take thought?

An. Becaufe their wits are oppreffed.

Que. Why are fooles full of Mony?

An. Becaufe tis their baby to play withall.

Que. Why do Mifers build faire houfes?

An. To mocke Beggars.

Que. Why doe Beggars loue their drinking?

An.

An. Becaufe it is an exercife of Idleneffe.
Que. why do Scolds loue fcolding?
An. Becaufe it is their naturall Mufique.
Que. why do not Theeues feare hanging?
An. Becaufe it is fo eafie a punifhment.
Que. why doe not the wicked feare God?
An. Becaufe they are to great with the Deuill.
Que. why are the vertuous moft happy.
An. Becaufe their ioyes are in heauen.

Cobs talke with Wifedome.

COme Wifedome, let me fpeake with thee
          a word or two,
Some bleffed Leffon reade to me
          what I fhall do:
What faift thou? Firft, that Chrift his Croffe
          muft be my fpeede:
My labour elfe would be but loffe,
          what ere I reade.
With Alpha then I muft begin
          to finde a friend:
To lead me from the way of finne
          to comforts end;
And in Omega reade the laft
          of all my loue,
Wherein my foule all forrow paft,
          her ioy may proue:
I muft not finne, I cannot chufe,
          ah wo is me,
To take the ill and good refufe,
          through want of thee.

E 3

In

Cobs talke with Wisedome.

In Youth I scorned thine aduice,
    now I am old,
I hold thy counsaile in more price
    then purest Gold:
Thou readst me patience, I confesse
    it easeth paine,
But little hope yet of redresse,
    thereby I gaine:
Thou readst me penitence for sinne,
    with sorrowes smart,
Oh there the sorrow doth begin
    that wounds my hart.
Thou readst me hope to heale my wound.
    with sorrowes teares;
But conscience makes my hart to swound,
    with sorrowes feares:
Thou readst me Faith, to hold my Hope
    on Mercies Grace,
But when that Faith the gate would ope,
    feare hides my face.
Thou readst me loue, the line of life
    that leades to blisse;
But hatefull sinne hath wrought the strife,
    where no loue is.
Thou readst me Truth yet in the word,
    that failes no trust:
But it doth onely Grace affoord
    vnto the iust.
Thou readst me Mercy, yet will heale
    the wounded hart:
To Mercy then let me appeale,
    to cure my smart.

                     And

And with true faithfull penitence,
    to sorrow so ;
That Hope with happy patience,
    to Heauen may go :
And there with Ioy at Mercies gate
    receiue that Grace,
Where neuer Soule that thou dost hate,
    may haue a place.

FINIS

www.ingramcontent.com/pod-product-compliance
Lightning Source LLC
Chambersburg PA
CBHW031450270326
41930CB00007B/938